ALSO BY FREDERICK FRANCK:

Days with Albert Schweitzer 1959

My Friend in Africa 1960

African Sketchbook 1961

My Eye Is in Love 1963

Outsider in the Vatican 1965

I Love Life 1967

Exploding Church 1968

Simenon's Paris 1969

The Zen of Seeing 1973

Pilgrimage to Now/Here 1973

An Encounter with Oomoto 1975

The Book of Angelus Silesius 1976

Every One, The Timeless Myth of Everyman Reborn 1978

Zen and Zen Classics, Selections from R.H. Blyth 1978

READERS:

Au Pays du Soleil 1958

Au Fil de l'Eau 1964

Croquis Parisiens 1969

Tutte le Strade Portano a Roma 1970

THE AWAKENED EYE

VINTAGE BOOKS, A DIVISION OF RANDOM HOUSE, NEW YORK

THE AWAKENED EYE

a companion volume to THE ZEN OF SEEING,

SEEING/DRAWING AS MEDITATION

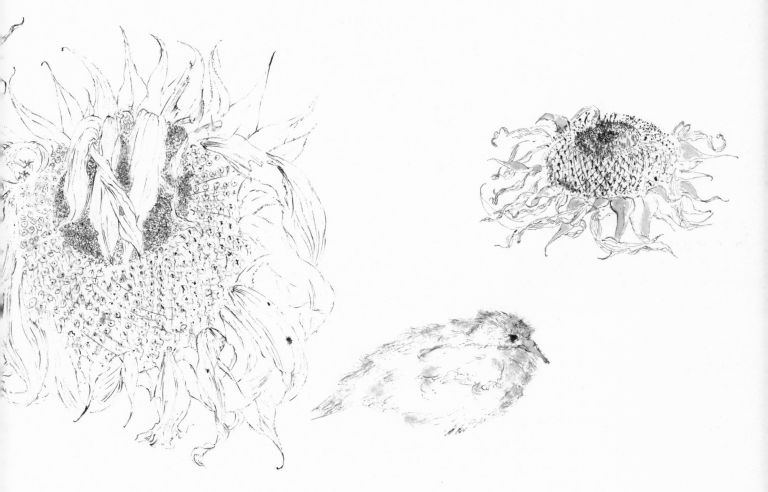

drawn and handwritten by

FREDERICK FRANCK

I wish to express my deep gratitude to Toinette Lippe —
exemplary editor, rare friend and counselor.

First Vintage Books Edition, September 1979
COPYRIGHT © 1979 by FREDERICK FRANCK
All rights reserved under International and Pan-American
Copyright Conventions. Published in the United States by
Random House, Inc., New York and simultaneously in Canada
by Random House of Canada Limited, Toronto.
Hardcover Edition published simultaneously
by Alfred A. Knopf Inc.

LIBRARY OF CONGRESS CATALOGING IN PUBLICATION DATA
Franck, Frederick, 1909 -
The awakened eye.
1. Franck, Frederick, 1909 -   2. Zen Buddhism.
I Title.
NC 139 . F 72 A4 1979 b   741'.092'4   79-4858
ISBN 0-394-74021-1

Manufactured in the United States of America

Quotations of Chinese and Japanese poetry and sayings are
often paraphrased according to the author's understanding of
them, from the works of R. H. Blyth and Daisetz T. Suzuki.

For Claske,
lover, friend,
absolute companion
on the Way.

FOREWORD

Once THE ZEN OF SEEING
– that book that was a love letter –
was written,
I returned to practice what
I had preached:
to "seeing/drawing as meditation."

Writing love letters
has its consequences:
If they are sincere
you have to live up to them.

I could only live up to mine
by deepening, intensifying

what I had written about;
I had to become my own
most diligent pupil,
(I don't say "disciple"
for I am not in the
guru business...)

I have this life—
of which most is gone—
to spend... or to waste...

So let me draw
and write, once more by hand,
person—to—person,
a second love letter to you.

When looking at the drawings
I hope you will realize
that not a single one was done
for the purpose of "illustrating"
something or other in the text.
I am not an illustrator...

These drawings were done
for one reason only:
to SEE before I die...

The text formed itself
around these drawings:
the words came out of the act,
the experience, of "seeing/drawing
as meditation."
In it I often speak of "I"
when actually I mean "you,"
for all that is human
we have in common...

The Awakened Eye

...One day, on the road to Norwood, I noticed a bit of ivy round a thorn stem... and proceeded to make a pencil study of it in my grey paper pocket book, carefully, liking it more and more as I drew. When it was done, I saw that I had virtually lost all my time since I was twelve years old, because no one had ever told me to draw what was really there!... I had never seen the beauty of anything, not even of a stone—how much less of a leaf!

John Ruskin (1819 - 1900)

"I have now seen the truth in this one instant," Yang-shan said. "But how should I apply it in everyday actions?" The Master replied: "All that is important is that you see things correctly. I don't talk about your everyday actions."

from The Transmission of the Lamp.

Since THE ZEN OF SEEING appeared, I have been asked to give workshops on "seeing/drawing as meditation" at many colleges, universities and other such institutions. Wonderful! But very soon I realized that I could conduct only a very limited number of these workshops if I did not want them to become a standardized, empty routine: an imposture. I found out that I could not give the same workshop twice. Each time it had to re-create itself completely in response to the particular mood, to the unspoken needs signaled by the group and by each person in the group with which I was working. Every workshop is either a fresh experiment in communication or is a bore to me and a useless fake for all in it! I also learned that I have to limit the number of participants in each workshop to at most twenty if each person is to receive the attention he needs.

As THE ZEN OF SEEING was a love letter, so each of these workshops seemed destined to become a kind of love affair with every new set of people, or rather, with each person in it, an intense but unsentimental involvement which came to include even the leaves and grasses that served as models during the long days of silent inwardness: I shared the being of the thistle or the blossoming branch I picked to draw. It looked me in the eye. I could not throw it out without qualms: it had become not-other.

Entering the forest, he moves not the grass,
entering the water, he makes not a ripple...

says an old Zen poem.

Since it is very unlikely that you took part in any workshop of mine, I shall try to let you experience one as vividly as I can, as a written workshop in "seeing/drawing as meditation." If, on the other hand, you did participate: may reading it give to you what writing this gave to me – a deeper awareness of the experience of seeing/drawing.

4

But first – before I forget, I must tell this story:

Once upon a time I was a little boy and my grandfather's house was full of treasures. Grandfather had an enormous roll-top desk of shiny mahogany that matched his bookcases with their beveled glass doors. In those bookcases stood all the classics in gold-embossed leather bindings, and an encyclopedia in which I diligently studied the fold-out "Human Anatomy – Female", until Anna, his housekeeper with her glassy – or perhaps glass – left eye and improbably high bosom, would slam it shut and snatch it away.

The greatest treasure of all, however, was the one Grandfather referred to as his "stereopticon." To this "stereopticon" I probably owe my way of life. The antique gadget consisted of twin lenses in a leather-covered housing, lined with red velvet. From this housing a kind of slide rule jutted forward, with a device at its end in which you placed twin photographs. Then, pressing the

velvet edge to your face, you saw through the lenses an oak,
not flat as in a picture, but all in the round, as a living presence.
For hours I could sit and watch the miraculous, living
three-dimensionality of cows in a meadow, lovers kissing
under a lilac bush, Queen Wilhelmina of the Netherlands on
her black steed, rotund ladies in stays and garter belt...
And so it came about that sometimes, when getting tired
on the long, lonely hikes I loved the fields, hills and
hedges began to look listless and flat in a dull two-dimension-
ality, I found I could order my eyes: "Now look through
the stereopticon!"
They would obey and the third dimension was at once restored.

Every sprig of grass came to life and stood there seperately in its own space; clumps of trees broke up into individual beings, each one springing from its own roots, deep in the earth.

People, when looked at through my mental stereoscope, underwent an extraordinary metamorphosis: each one became the impressively unique, mysterious being he never expected himself to be... That which, when merely looked at, was mailman, poplar or squirrel became — when seen stereoptically — unnameable, ineffable.

I found my trick of stereoscopic seeing such a precious secret that I never mentioned it to anyone. But I practiced it as often as I could, and discovered that seeing things and beings stereoptically could take the place of a lot of thinking "about" them.

I now realize that Grandfather's stereoscope was the mute Master who initiated me into seeing, gave me the first hint of the potentiality of my everyday eye to become an awakened eye, an eye that can do more than merely look at things in order to recognize them, an eye that can really SEE the Ten Thousand Things, not just-as-they-are, but such-as-they-are: in their meaning, their truth and totality. It gave me a first taste of contemplation.

When all looks dull and déjà-vu, I can still command my eye to see stereoptically, and make it awaken from its routine slumber.

There is no other valid reason for drawing than the awareness of the eye awakening from its half-sleep. There is – I am convinced – no other good reason for art, all the art-popes and theories notwithstanding...

The stereopticon experience did more than open up a contemplative way of seeing. It had – I feel – a great deal to do with my becoming an incurable image-maker (isn't that more precise and less pretentious than "artist"?). But perhaps even more crucial was an experience that had come earlier, an experience as unique as it must be universal, for I believe each one of us can recall one that is similar. Unless you can recollect such an experience of your own after reading mine, you may have drifted further away from yourself than you realize.

This is what happened:

I was five years old. My mother and a friend I was expected to address as "Aunt" had taken us children to a modest little tea garden with swings and seesaws on the edge of our small town on the Dutch-Belgian border. It sported the elegant French name of "Les Champs Elysées": the Elysian Fields — the Celestial Fields of Bliss... I can still see and hear the trio that was playing on the rickety bandstand: the thin, sorrowful violinist in his patent leather shoes, the bald, rotund pianist, the bosomy lady in white tulle, a moaning cello clamped between her short, plump thighs.

The other children were still swinging and seesawing when I got bored, and as mother and the pseudo-aunt with her long nose were absorbed in the music — which did not prevent them from chattering rapturously in whispers — I saw my chance to escape across a narrow stream, and found myself in a sun-drenched meadow. I lay down in the fragrant, swaying grass, tall enough to make me unfindable, and listened to the trio far away. Then, suddenly there was a loud zooming close to my ear and I was terrified: a velvety bee circled around my head, almost touching it.

But ignoring me, it sat down on a hairy purple flower that was so close to my head that it looked huge and vague, and started to suck... At that moment something happened: all my fear evaporated, but so did bee and sun and grass... and I. For at that instant sunlight and sky, grasses, bee and I merged, fused, became one — yet remained sun and sky and grass and bee and I. It lasted for a heartbeat, an hour, a year... Then, as abruptly, I was I again, but filled with an indescribable bliss— were they not Elysian Fields?

The trio was still playing the tune that I remember to this day, and I can whistle it for you anytime you wish...
I had probably come as close to reality as I ever was to come in this life.

The older I get, the more faithful I seem to become to the child I then was. It is this child who draws and writes this book, trusting that the child in you will find it true.
I often wonder if any one of us ever becomes an adult, for I have noticed that as people get older, when they "mature," as it is said, they either become wonderfully childlike, or else despicably infantile...

The Stereopticon and the episode in the meadow I now see as the first inklings of Zen experience, of awakening, of KENSHO, which predestined me to become who I am now. My parents may have coaxed, almost coerced me into becoming a doctor, but as soon as I could afford to — or rather, dare to — I hung my white coat on a hook and slammed the office door behind me. For once we have experienced it, we must seek always to recapture this timeless moment, however far we are led astray by the buffetings and temptations of life. I found I could indeed recapture it at will: the discipline, the technique to awaken the eye I called SEEING/DRAWING.

"If we take eternity to mean not infinite temporal duration, but timelessness, the eternal life belongs to those who live in the present," says Wittgenstein.

While seeing/drawing a beech tree, a leaf, a face, I see it "through the stereopticon" in three dimensions. But now a fourth dimension has been added. Not only do I see it in space, I see it in time: in its time. The form of a tree is its time: Seen in space, its pattern is that of its growing, its being, its time... The face I draw changes its feature play constantly. The leaf I just picked is already going limp, then I see it shrivel. While seeing/drawing I see each thing living its own time, as I am living my time, my life-time. The awakened eye becomes utterly aware of the fleetingness of all that passes before it, of this eye still seeing, of this hand still moving, still tracing...

For to the awakened
eye no thing remains
a mere thing. It reveals
itself to be, instead of an object, an EVENT in the
timeless abyss of time, an event of unfathomable
meaning that happens to take place more or less simultaneously
with the event I call "Me". In the language of Zen this state of
no-thingness, of selflessness, is called MU (literally it means
"no"), in which I become an empty vessel, filled by what the
eye sees. Drawing the rosehips I let them flow through
this MU, let them precipitate themselves onto the paper,
as if without any "thinking", any interference on my part.
For these moments to happen I have lived sixty-some years...

R.H. Blyth speaks of MU as a state of absolute spiritual
poverty, and says that to the extent a person understands
"Blessed are the poor in spirit," he understands MU.

Now to our "written workshop"! It is not intended as a more or less lively or entertaining description, but as much as possible an equivalent of the real thing, which I hope will move you to grab your pencil and to start seeing/drawing the Ten Thousand Things — that are not just "things" and so to make contact with the Seer, the artist within, the contact with the fullness of Life!

Imagine you have registered for the workshop and that you are one of the people who come trickling in around nine. You make yourself known to the person who receives you and then you sit quietly on the floor, forming a semicircle with the others in the silence that has been requested from the very start. It is 9³⁰ a.m. now. All are present and I am called. My introduction to the day's work varies each time, but it might run something like this:

Good Morning!
This is not going to be just a "workshop." Actually it is intended as a "retreat" — not one of passive introspection, but of a return to being in fully alert, awake contact with what is outside

ourselves, with what is not_I: with that living world of which
we are part.

The two main elements of this retreat are: SEEING and SILENCE.
Both are equally important. The silence is indispensable to the
seeing. To see, there must be silence at last, inner silence
and outer silence.

When all the usual din and chatter are switched off,
you are at last alone, able to meet yourself,
and to see those around you in their
silent aloneness.

You have probably already sized up the other people in this
group; you have already appraised one another. You will
find these appraisals evaporating during the day as will
some of your other prejudices and assumptions: for instance,

that you know what a clump of grass looks like! You will see one another in undivided wakefulness, in a mood of meditative activity that is very close to, maybe equivalent to, wordless prayer. You will see the other in his humanness and feel closer than if you had talked all day. Here, today, we simply are who we are, you as well as I. Hence let's avoid introductions and all the smalltalk that goes with them. Our names don't really matter, nor "where we're from"... If we knew where we were from, we'd know where we are going... we would have solved the riddle of our existence...

Seeing/drawing is neither a pastime nor one of the fifty-seven varieties of what presents itself as "self-expression," which is all too often mere ego-indulgence, characteristic of that market place that calls itself "the art world." Today we are not going to fabricate art objects: the market is glutted with framable objects for the next few generations...

If this day is to be of real value to you, it must literally be an eye-opener: an experiment in seeing through drawing. We are not going to aim at being "creative"... To be "creative" is so very fashionable that it has become another compulsion, another sadly competitive game. Nor will we compete in being "original" in the sense of trying to do something that no one has ever done before, because a thing which resembles nothing that preceded it is most likely to be... nothing...
I have to stress this because so much writing on art and art appreciation has the awful effect of making us distrust our own eyes... TODAY WE SHALL TRUST OUR OWN EYES ONLY!

Instead of the pleasures of so-called "self-expression," you will discover a greater one: the joy of letting a leaf, a branch, express itself, its being, through you. In order to reach that point you'll have to allow yourself to see that which you are drawing, whether leaf, plant or weed, as the most important thing on earth, worthy of your fullest, deepest attention.

"ATTENTION! ATTENTION!" is the watchword for today!

There is a quite other satisfaction I can promise you. It will come at the end of the day, when you compare your first drawings of this morning with the ones that will come quite spontaneously later this afternoon. There will be a difference as if you had been drawing not for seven hours, but for at least a week, or even weeks...

If you enter wholeheartedly into the spirit of this retreat, you may well experience something of what Zen is, even if I won't do much talking about Zen, except to say that ZEN IS THAT WHICH BRINGS US IN DIRECT CONTACT WITH THE INNER WORKINGS OF LIFE.

Zen meditation, zazen, is the traditional discipline by which this contact with the innermost workings of Life, with the True Self, is made.

There are, however, also other Zen disciplines, spoken of as "the Ways": archery, Nō play, tea ceremony, calligraphy. For particular temperaments these are equivalents, alternative disciplines to zazen—"yogas," one may well say—which, if seriously practiced, are indeed Ways to realization, to awakening.

For me _ and perhaps for you _ seeing/drawing is such a Way, a "Zenless Zen", without Oriental trappings, kimonos, folklore or even bamboo brushes, a Western Way leading to the awakening of the eye for those to whom sitting motionlessly for long periods does not come naturally.

At the end of the day you are likely to be dead-tired: for seeing with pure, undivided attention is _ and not only for the beginner _ very exhausting. And I too will be just as tired. For all day I'll have to see through your eyes. I'll have to see what you see. I'll have to see through twenty pairs of eyes! But even more: I'll have to identify intuitively and totally with the temperament, with the "given" of each one of you, with your particular muscle coordination, your "aptitude" (not to use that vague, misleading word "talent"). For if I do not, I shall ask you to do what goes against your nature, instead of bringing you closer to it, making you aware of your true nature _ of Who you might really be.

Actually, seeing/drawing confronts me constantly with the person I pretend _ to myself and others _ to be, the person I may imagine myself to be, the one I strive to be. It makes me realize who I am definitely NOT _ which is vastly more important!

This may make it clear why I deny having anything to "teach" you.
At most I can help you liberate what lies hidden, untapped.
If I make some remark on the way you draw, it is never in
order to teach you some technique, some trick or other,
but to point at some deficiency in your SEEING and
to stimulate your capacity for experience, for greater
openness.

We humans can teach each other many things, except the ones
that really matter and which each of us has to discover by
himself. Hence how-to books on drawing lead us astray and
are as dangerous as how-to books on lovemaking. Both have
much in common, and what they have in common cannot be

learned by rote, but can only be realized by de-programming, by unlearning, by seeing—for instance—what it is to be a blade of grass. Or rather: that _a_ blade of grass does not exist — that only this particular blade of grass exists; and that "_a_" man, "_a_" woman are figments of the imagination, only this particular man or woman is real. Drawing the Ten Thousand Things is a way of loving, of being in love with life by seeing each thing in its singularity.

Whatever the improvement I predicted between your first and your last drawings: do realize that this one-day experiment is no more than an initiation (or, as someone said, "a one-shot therapy against blindness"). If you continue, however, you will have found your Way, you may well be _on_ your Way!

Am I pretending to promise you instant enlightenment? Hardly! The great Zen scholar D.T. Suzuki writes that the word "Enlightenment" in Buddhist literature is often interpreted as "mind attains the Unconditioned"... He explains that SEEING is the enlightenment experience, the seeing in which the opposition between subject and object has been overcome, in which you become what you see. This is precisely what happens in seeing/drawing. In order to draw a leaf, you have to <u>become</u> that leaf.

He also makes the surprising statement that according to Mahayana Buddhism there is no real opposition, or incompatibility, between the True Self and the ego and that the ego — the little isolated self — is not "annihilated" at all in Enlightenment, but that the inner life has now attained such an infinite range that "the enlightened person's desire contains no more snares, no poison". The ego has become harmless to other beings, it has lost its sting, it has "turned around at its base," has come to see itself to be:
NEITHER I NOR OTHER

Enlightenment then is simply sanity! The sanity in which I see my real situation in the living fabric of all that exists. It is the ultimate sanity that has also been called sanctity.

To my amazement I found that the discipline of seeing/drawing combines aspects of both surviving schools of Zen, now so compelling to us Westerners, which for centuries have opposed each other. They are known as Soto Zen and Rinzai Zen.

According to Dōgen, the sage who imported Soto Zen into Japan from China in the 13th Century, the practice of zazen is by itself the manifestation of the enlightenment which is the very core of our being human, however concealed it may be under thick layers of the busy-ness, the obsessions, of the little self. For the "Me" imagines itself to be permanent and autonomous, without realizing it is a wretched chimera which has been genetically programmed from the moment of Conception, and then from the instant of birth conditioned further by tribe, nation, sect, by all the forces of the culture it grows up in.

In Christianity it is said that when I truly pray, it is not I who pray but the Spirit that dwells in me. In Soto Zen the practice of sitting in "silent illumination" is not seen as "my" activity but as that of the Buddha Nature: zazen itself IS enlightenment. According to Rinzai Zen this view goes counter to the very spirit of Zen. Rinzai (9th Century) goes as far as to say that "trying to attain Buddhahood (awakening, Enlightenment) by merely sitting cross-legged in meditation is tantamount to murdering the Buddha".

Not that Rinzai Zen rejects sitting in silent meditation — on the contrary; but here zazen does not consist in tranquil serenity, but in focusing the field of one's consciousness exclusively on a central problem or "Koan," to the extent that the meditator's mind becomes literally transformed into the riddlesome Koan which his intellect can never solve... until at long last enlightenment breaks through in a flash of insight. There are over a thousand such Koan in Zen, each one of which — couched in paradoxical, often nonsensical and arational language — may ultimately reveal itself as a crystallization of the life problem, an epitome of Zen insight into Ultimate Reality. Without going into details — there are now dozens of books on the subject — I found to my astonishment that not only do I, while seeing/drawing, experience something very akin to Soto's "silent illumination," but that at the same time THE TREE I AM DRAWING — IN THAT POINTED WAKEFULNESS IN WHICH NOT A TRACE IS LEFT OF CALCULATIVE SURFACE — THINKING — BECOMES THE KOAN WITH WHICH I IDENTIFY TOTALLY. Every new drawing of the tree becomes a further step toward the solution of the Koan.

Each one of the trees I have drawn was the one Jōshū's famous Koan speaks of: When asked by a monk "What is Ultimate Reality?", Jōshū pointed and replied: "The Cypress tree in the front yard."

26

Jōshū's tree stands in my own front yard, as it stood in the
park where, as a boy, I embraced and kissed it stealthily, when
no one was looking... I saw my neighbor cut down Jōshū's
tree, just to try out his new power saw. He was proud of
it as he is proud of having shot a little rabbit, or even an old
carp near the waterfall, for he does not know, as Chuang Tzu
knew," the joy of fishes, as I walk along the river." Nor does
he see, as Wanshi saw:
" Just pick up anything you like: in everything it is so
nakedly manifested..."

Both Soto and Rinzai methods are upaya, "skillful means", to shock us out of our delusional state of half-sleep, disciplines that aim at helping us to de-condition, to de-program ourselves, to free us from the bondage of that primeval ignorance called avidya with which we are burdened. Avidya is that which distorts and blurs our vision of self and of the world, for it assumes the "Me" to be the measure of all things. To be liberated from the pathology of avidya (which in Sanskrit literally means not-knowing, ig-norance, in the sense of un-intelligence, i.e. stupidity!) is to be awakened or enlightened, to see realistically, to find one's true place in the organic Whole, to see with the awakened eye.

When the Zen master Satcho was asked where the demarcation line lies between this vale of tears and the earthly paradise of fulfillment and peace, he answered: "The eye is the demarcation line." Paradise, for Zen, is accessible now and here, for it is our everyday world, but perceived by the awakened eye.

"For long years I have been a bird in a cage;
today I am flying along with the clouds..."
sang a Zen poet.

near Amsterdam

However hard you may search for it,
You will never be able to grasp it
You can only BECOME it.   (IKKYU)

There have been Westerners who had something to say about SEEING
that equals Zen insights. Emerson felt himself "become a
transparent eyeball." "I am nothing," he exclaimed, "I see all! The
currents of Universal Being circulate through me: I am part and
parcel of God." And Heidegger: "The field of vision is something
open, but its openness is not due to our looking."
Jesus, however, said more simply: "The eye is the candle of the
body"...When he made the blind man SEE, the blindfold he tore
away was the blindfold of avidya. The man, I suppose, had been
able to look all along, he just had never seen.

When, at last, while seeing/drawing, you see for the first time what all your life you have only looked at and recognized, it reveals itself to be of inconceivable intricacy. The commonplace becomes uncommon. An ordinary patch of grass suddenly discloses all the mystery of Being. As the Zen expression has it: It becomes "a sixteen-foot-high Buddha."

When I am totally absorbed in drawing it, and have become leaf or grass, when the split between I-as-subject and It-as-object is bridged, it becomes more than just a huge golden Buddha — which is, after all, only a dead piece of sculpture. What I am now in touch with is no dead artifact but the process of life itself. The leaf's budding, unfurling, wilting and dying are my own! For however short a span, IT — instead of Me — has become the center of my universe. It is no longer a thing observed: but an ever-changing, ever-fleeting mystery, which, like myself, flashes past at the speed of light. Then, in this flashing Now, I may glimpse Reality, I may recognize the Self, that Original Face I share with all that is; I may glimpse the Buddha Nature: the Pearl of Great Price.

Each stroke, each dot your pencil makes on the paper is A MEASURE OF YOUR AWARENESS, of the quality of your awareness. And this it is my task to point out during your work, so that later you may discern for yourself, in whatever you draw, the quality of your awareness without self-deception, and continue to discard all pretensions, all stylizations, devices and short cuts.

Recently when I saw an exhibition of ice-age art, it struck me how close those horses, reindeer and human faces painted and carved on rock walls are to what I call seeing/drawing. Our paleolithic ancestors were not sophisticated, ego-ridden "artists," they neither copied nor "described" their world. Their eye was totally involved in, identified with, the beings it saw and which their hand traced. They too were seeing/drawing! It was as if a direct line connected these primeval images with the clear-eyed imagery of the ancient Chinese Zen painters. They share that "flash of livingness" of which the 17th Century painter and Zen master Hakuin spoke...

One glance at a drawing discloses the moment at which all efforts of the little self-obsessed ego stopped, at which looking became seeing and the hand started to move by itself in unison with what the eye perceived.

It is fascinating during these workshops to pinpoint this moment. For hours I have been watching you draw the branching of plants and flowers as if they were mechanical joints, as if branches were nailed or screwed to the stem! Then, suddenly, the joints you draw come to life: the stem swells almost imperceptibly where the branch is about to wrest itself free, guarded by a paper-thin sheath... Now you have seen! You have become that branching! Seeing/drawing has become wide-eyed Contemplation...

To sum up:

Yisan said to a monk pining for enlightenment:

"I have nothing to give you. But if I would try, you would be right to laugh in my face, for whatever I could tell you is my own; it could never be yours."

Next: I must make sure you understand that in this retreat there will be no meditation apart from the seeing/drawing: your seeing/drawing IS your meditation! Also: that although I promised you the progress in your drawing you will almost certainly see at the end of this day, it is quite secondary in importance to your having experienced that true seeing which will enrich you for the rest of your life. Hui Neng's "The meaning of life is to see" is a mantra I find confirmed each time I draw...

Last of all: Don't be disappointed if there will be as little talk "about" Zen as I can manage. If I spent all day talking about Zen, it would bring you no closer to experiencing it, and my hope for today is that you may experience something of Zen without labeling it as such. Seeing/drawing is no panacea for the ills and sufferings of the world: it just heals the split between myself and that which surrounds me...

Now, before we start, here are a few practical hints:

Sit at least six feet apart. Put your drawing board on your knees. Begin with something "simple," a leaf for instance. Take it in your hand and observe it closely for a few minutes. Then put it in a corner of your drawing paper, close your eyes... try to visualize it. Hold your pencil loosely and let it rest on the paper. After a few minutes of trying to visualize the leaf, open your eyes. You may now begin to SEE the leaf, and while keeping fully concentrated on it, let your pencil start to move. As it moves, have the feeling that the pencil point is gently caressing the contours of the leaf: the outline that goes around it, as well as the cross-contours that go across it.

Don't let your pencil move unless it is "in contact" with these contours. Let every mark on the paper be a witness to what your eye sees. Allow the image on your retina to set off the reflex arc that goes directly from your eye, through your body, to the fingers that hold the pencil,

SO THAT THE PENCIL BECOMES LIKE A SEISMOGRAPHIC NEEDLE

Corfu I -'79

THAT REGISTERS THE INNER TREMORS, THE "VIBRATIONS" OF YOUR SEEING.

There is no thinking, judging, labeling in this reflex arc: it goes from the eye to the hand and skips the thinking, judging, discriminating brain: just allow the reflex to work, to take over! All progress in drawing is the refinement of this reflex arc. This may sound enigmatic to you now. But I'll remind you of it constantly and clarify it in practice. Don't be surprised: in the beginning your concentration span will be short. When your attention flags, stop for a moment.
Above all: don't continue to scribble while your eye freewheels...

While drawing I often find myself "talking to my pencil" to keep my concentration keen: "Here it twists this way," I hear myself say, "and here it folds under very gently," and so on. It is simply a way of keeping my attention taut.

If at the start your line runs off the paper, don't worry. Soon your hand will adapt itself to the available space. And although your eye is focused on the leaf you are drawing, there is no prohibition against checking on what is happening on your paper once in a while: as long as your eye's concentration on that leaf is unbroken.

There will be moments during the day when you will feel desperate to the point of wanting to quit. You may even tell yourself that you are bored. I have found out that these moments of despair often come when at last the ego gives up trying. It is the point where real seeing, where "meditation" can start.

Don't sign your drawings; just number them in sequence. I'll come around to each person many times. But when I talk to you, please do not take it as an invitation to conversation! Just listen. Don't explain or try to justify why you are doing what! If you have a question, I'll answer it, of course, but please: no talk. I'll just put my finger to my lips to remind you that this is a day of silence.

Above all: don't try to argue with me. If you insist on "doing your
own thing" during this workshop, you will be wasting this day.
Do your own thing tomorrow!
I have done more than enough talking... And yet, since this
is after all a "Zen of seeing" retreat, I feel I should say just
one more word about Zen. And so I shall end with a paraphrase
of the celebrated description of Zen attributed to Bodhidharma,
the man who brought Zen from India to China some fifteen
hundred years ago.
This is what I understand Bodhidharma as saying:

From heart to heart it is transmitted,
it cannot be expressed in words and letters.
It is a special transmission
—independent of all scriptures and sacred texts—
of That Which Matters...
It is a direct pointing at the human heart-mind
that makes us see and be in contact with
our deepest nature, that specifically Human
nature that is spoken of as Buddha Nature,
as the Original Face, as the Essence of Mind,
as the Indwelling Spirit...

And now, after a short ritual, we'll start our working day.

The ritual that follows is very simple. It came to me from nowhere and imposed itself. Without it I feel the workshop to be incomplete. Each time I have to overcome a certain shyness, am tempted to skip it, for I despise theatricality. Yet each time it confirms itself again as indispensable.

I ask the participants to form a circle and I stand in its center. Starting with the one I happen to face, I look him in the eye and make a deep bow, hands folded before my chest. Almost without exception, the one I bow to will bow back. Our eyes meet again for an instant or two. I repeat this greeting to each one in turn and in this momentary contact

I am aware of taking in each person totally. The quality of
the bow, of this quiet moment of recognition, tells me almost more
than I have a right to know. It is probably mutual...
"Now we have greeted one another as we really are. We have
seen each other. Let's start!"

For me this ritual is expression and confirmation of
my absolute respect for, and acceptance of, each one
as he is: as a private, inviolate, once-occurring
person. Every mistake, every confusion, every short
cut, every failing this person is going to show
during the work, is one I have committed a hundred
times myself, and still find myself sliding back into.
And it is remarkable that everyone seems to
understand the ritual — although the deep bow
is hardly part of the social graces of Ohio
or Michigan...

They sit on the floor, drawing pads on their knees, and are observing their leaves. A few who have done yoga sit in meditation posture, but I have not noticed that this makes any difference in their intensity of perception. Now they close their eyes.

By and by as they begin to draw, watching every motion in the circle, I start my rounds. I see how one is beginning to draw somewhere in the lower corner of her paper. Another has chosen a much-too-complicated branch for a first attempt, a third flies off with a furiously nervous scribble all over the place. A fourth one seems to be playing "artist at work" for a nonexistent movie camera. Very quietly, but immediately, I respond to all that happens: I replace the too-complicated branch, soothe the nervous one, focus attention, point out, suggest.

There is no "system" in what I do. I simply respond minute by minute to what I feel is needed, and cannot explain it further: I have the physical sensation of looking through each one's eyes, of drawing with each one's hand. I have noticed how even my voice changes: I hear myself sound a bit ironical at times, very hesitant at others, or authoritarian, or tender, or coaxing... I may stop much longer and more frequently at one person than another, with some a mere gesture suffices...

"Don't hurry!," I hear myself say, or "You have drawn a good deal, haven't you? You are performing the tricks you learned! Try to forget what you think you know: just SEE!"

To a horsy woman I say: "Caress that leaf! You are giving it a massage!" To an elderly nun: "Make love to that daisy, Sister!" And I keep whispering all over: "Lighter! Lighter!! Hold that pencil lightly!..." For in the beginning the lines tend to be stiff and heavy like iron wire: diaphanous petals become slabs of cast metal...

"Don't use that heavy marker, it is useless for our purpose," I explain to the film star, and give him a sharp HB pencil. At once he falls out of his star role; a few minutes later he is on his way, tongue between his teeth, concentrating on his milkweed pod... Another great-stage-personality-by-inclination acts blasé: "I find it rather boring, to be frank," she whispers.

"It is! It is! If you see nothing but that, life becomes indeed excruciatingly boring!" I say, pointing at the blackened scribble that has little resemblance to anything, least of all to the subtly white mushroom lying on her drawing paper.

"Now let's try!" I sit down with her: "Look at this miracle..."
Another one has been fumbling for almost an hour with the branch of pine he had chosen.

"You just don't seem to be a pine branch person... go and pick something that really strikes you." He returns with a cluster of withered oak leaves, immensely more complex, more difficult to draw. Still, the leaves are taking shape quickly on the paper.

"How do I make that leaf turn up at the edge?"

"There is no how-to trick to it! Just see and let your pencil follow what you see. Let it draw itself!"

The fumbling has stopped. The edges start to turn up.

There is always one who says:

"I wish I could watch you draw! Can I watch you draw?"

"I can't draw with someone watching me, sorry!"

"Why?"

"Because I'm aware of your watching instead of being aware of what I am seeing/drawing."

"But I'll keep very still. Please let me watch you draw!"

"O.K. then: if I can watch you make love, or watch you pray... I'll keep very still..."

46

Round and round I go, sharpening a pencil here and there, for only the sharp pencil point ever acts as it should, honestly—as the seismographic needle that registers the inward tremors.

"This is purely an experiment in seeing, not in picture making. So please no blackening even if you call it "shading". For our purpose today "shading" is not drawing. It is rather painting with a pencil, and it will interfere with your rigorous seeing...Today your line itself has to catch every form, even to EXPRESS every form!"

"There is no line in Nature," argues the one with the Ph.D., whose leaves are shapeless black blotches, done with the flat side of a pencil.

"No, indeed! Nor is there color in nature! Without my human eye the grass is not green, the sky is not blue. Without scales the elephant is weightless...There is not a trace of solidity in this whirling of electrons you are sitting on. Still, aren't you sitting comfortably on it?"

I risk being found sentimental, pointing at a hole chewed out of a leaf by a caterpillar:

"Look! It is not punched out by a machine. It is chewed out. Just imagine it is chewed out of your arm! It hurts!"

I give a shriveled, dry leaf to the blasé one: "How about drawing this? Here you see life and death; just allow yourself to see..." She is working assiduously now, no longer bored.

I am responding constantly to stated and unstated questions, doubts, distractions. Sometimes it is disquieting: a young woman who from the start looked strangely preoccupied is drawing a birch branch. I see her at work on one of the leaves.

"That is not just a dark spot," I say, "don't you see that crusty thickening, all swollen? Let that express itself in your drawing! Must be a tumor..." She looks at me in horror and, frowning, goes on drawing the leaf. It becomes extraordinarily convincing and vivid.

"Wonderful," I say on my next stop, "that's it!" She whispers: "May I say something? This morning I got a phone call. My best friend was taken to the hospital for a sudden operation: a tumor! At first I didn't want to come, I was so upset. Then you mentioned about the tumor... How could you know? Or do you say that often?"

"No, never... It _is_ strange, I have never said that before..."

"Somehow," she says, "it made me face what happened. I had been so upset, and while drawing that awful spot, I became quiet..."

"I'll tell you a story about becoming quiet, if you remind me of it after we are all through..."

"I just can't copy that clover!"

"Seeing/drawing is NOT copying nature! It is responding to nature in full awareness; to the way nature expresses itself in that clover. Don't give a thought to 'copying'.
SEE that clover, become it, and it will draw itself...'

It did start to draw itself, quite beautifully and miraculously.

"Yes! This is it! Really alive, don't you agree?"

"Oh yes; but how did I do it? I don't know how I did it!"

"You didn't do it. Your hand just obeyed your eye. Only your hand could do this particular drawing: it is as much yours as your fingerprint!"

"If the doors of perception were cleansed,
everything would appear to man as it is —
Infinite," says Blake. And Eckhart:
"ANY FLEA AS IT IS IN GOD, IS NOBLER THAN
THE HIGHEST ANGEL IN HEAVEN."
Any clover!

Around noon we stop for a silent lunch, but I encourage
my group — yes, by now I feel it as MY group, they are no
longer strangers — to make that lunch break as long or as short
as they wish, and to go back to drawing as soon as they feel like it.
By now I try to show how even the lightest lines can be varied, accented,
to suggest three-dimensionality, how by varying the pressure on the
pencil ever so slightly a line can become expressive, and that
this variation in intensity is not a trick but truly the result of
clear, intensive seeing.

Around 3 p.m. I know I can expect the best drawings of the day. All the
surface agitation, all pretenses have been shed. The anxieties, the
all-too-hard trying of the beginning hours are gone. Eyes and
hands have steadied; in even the most unsure one I feel the rising

of confidence. The room radiates quiet... It is about this time that on my rounds I can so often point at a spot where the stem of leaf or fruit branches out: "Now! See! HERE THE MEDITATION STARTS! All that went before was practice, preparation! You see?!"

There is not the slightest doubt: here a living, a growing, a groping is expressing itself. The branching is no longer a joint made by a welder or carpenter.

At this time of the day a great similarity in quality is noticeable in all these drawings, yet each one clearly has its own handwriting, cannot be confused with anyone else's, is the precipitation of one distinct person's seeing: authentic.

By 4 p.m. the group begins to wilt. Is that woman over there crying? "What is the matter? Are you not feeling well?"

"Oh, it is so tremendous!" she sobs, pointing at the minute leaves that protect the tiny bud of a flower, "why can't I get that? I just can't!" I look at her drawing. "But this is wonderful! What a leap you made. Look how this drawing differs from all you did before! You have been drawing a birth!"

It is the despair I know all too well, even after all these years... When what is before your eye starts to reveal itself as the

ineffable manifestation of the universe, when rustling
grasses start to whisper gravely and rocks start to sing,
when the model's naked body suddenly is no longer body,
no longer beautiful or ugly, you are overcome: simply because
it is, because it moves, because it walks,
because it speaks... Infinite miracle
to which your drawing
never does justice...

The iron man sings
the stone woman dances

says a Zen koan. I had to solve this koan
by drawing thousands of men and women
in and out of their clothes, until I knew:

"AH, THIS IS IT! YES! THIS!"

"Tell the story about getting quiet," she said, after I had hung the "anonymous exhibition" that ends the workshop and that gives me the opportunity to "read" that quality of awareness I spoke about, to clarify once more what happened in the course of the day. Since the drawings are unsigned there is no embarrassment: only the person who drew it knows whom I talk about. They go around, amazed at what happened between the drawings done at the beginning and at the end of the day. Sometimes it seems as if months of serious study have passed in these few hours.

"I just can't believe I did this! Never thought I could really draw!"
    "So my prediction came true?"
    "It certainly did! But how do I go on from here?"
    "Just go on as you did today for fifteen years or so! Seeing/Drawing is not for hobbyists. It is a Way, a discipline. Each deepened awareness leads to the next level of awareness. Instead of becoming blunted and cynical by existence, your sensitivity will become ever keener. Looking through my drawings of ten, fifteen years ago – that is, the ones I found good enough to keep, for I throw out many more than I keep – I find them crude... It is not that I find a better technique in the more recent ones: I find a greater truth, a greater faithfulness to what I really see.

AD MAIOREM DEI GLORIAM

To establish the eye-to-hand reflex seems to be a matter of
grace. To refine it is a matter of constant practice in which the
eye becomes ever more Sensitized and the hand ever more
Submissive, more responsive to the image
on the retina.

If I don't draw for even a week, I feel I must start from scratch, for I have lost what it may take hours or days of painful effort to recover: that state of grace in which the reflex takes over from the straining ego. So how do you go on from here? By drawing every day, if even for half an hour, by drawing everything, anything: the beans you are going to cook, a fried egg, your grandfather, your own toes..."

"Now tell the story," she insisted, and exhausted as I was, I had to tell of the morning a few years ago when I was driving to New York from my home in Warwick. I had gone a few miles when I switched on my radio for the news.
"Explosions are heard as far as Tel Aviv...huge columns of tanks are crossing the Suez Canal..." it said.
My heart seemed to skip: "Another war!"

Once more a flashback. I was not in school yet...A mile south of my hometown, across the Belgian border, the First World War had started. Stiff with horror I saw the flaming town of Visé from our attic window. The constant booming of the big guns was to accompany my childhood... It was the beginning of the barbaric sequence of bloodbaths that has continued ever since.

"I've had it!", I heard myself shout.
For a split second I was suicidal,
almost drove my car into a tree.
Instead I stopped.

On my left a meadow
was gently rising toward a blue
sky with white clouds, a meadow full of purple and white
autumn flowers. Where meadow and sky met stood a
fringe of feathery trees. I took my sketchbook, climbed
halfway up the slope, sat down and started to draw the
grasses, thistles, flowers, the wispy trees.
"Behold, all flesh is as the grass" from Brahms' Requiem came
back to me... After a while I noticed that my agitation had
ebbed away. Not the sadness, nor the despair, but the
turmoil and the black anger. I had found a still point, my
center.

Still you are here...still here: meadow, grass,
Queen Anne's lace...beloved Earth!
I am still here! My eyes still see!
I and this meadow, I and these grasses...
we are NOT-TWO...
Escape from reality?
Oh no!! Escape into Reality!
IN THE MIDST OF FOLLY AND
TERROR: THE LIFELINE
TO THE SOURCE RETRIEVED.

It is this flash of realization, of not_two_ness, that is both the
center and the end point of our human experience. In every
seed of every weed, in the knee_joint of a dead wasp's leg,
the structure of The Whole of Reality is laid bare for those
who have eyes to see.

Our brain filters out the overwhelming poignancy of this
Structure of Reality, of the Divine, as it manifests itself in all
that is. The eye, however, when it awakens, sees all things as
"unseparated" from itself, to speak with Eckhart.

And thus seeing/drawing becomes an almost continuous
hymn to life: "Beloved Earth!"

I used to love drawing France more than Italy, Holland more
than either, and all of these more than America.
This was long ago, and I don't know how it happened, but no
longer partial, my eyes now love the spot my feet happen
to stand on.

Paris '79

At the end of one of these workshops (it was at the Koinonia Community in Baltimore) an art teacher said: "I realized today that I was totally brainwashed in art school. Today was an antidote! I don't want to stop now! Why can't we go on for a week? Seriously, couldn't we draw like this for a week or a month?"

It gave me an idea. Yes, we'd have our seeing/drawing marathon, based on THE ZEN OF SEEING. But this time we would draw "from life" or from what they call "the Nude". But I called it "Confrontation with The Human..."

We found over a dozen enthusiasts to participate, and as many people willing to pose for us — black, white and Oriental, male and female, fat and thin, as young as a seven-week-old baby and as old as a couple of very senior citizens.

We were going to draw, not for a month — that was not very practical — but for four days, and would draw for nine hours each day: three hours in the morning, three in the afternoon, and three hours in the evening. Only after the evening session would we sit together over a glass of wine and, if not too exhausted, talk about the experiences of the day. The group would be limited to people who had at least some experience of drawing the human figure.

In my introduction to the workshop I urged everyone not to see the people who were going to pose for us as just "models," as if they were animated manikins, machines of bones and muscles, for this is what the "clinical material" of life-classes is usually assumed to be.

To see the living body (which as William Blake realized is the visible aspect of the soul) as "ovoid volume summaries", "surface tensions", "space systems", "plastic activities" and such (I copy this jargon from a recent textbook on drawing) reduces the human being before your eye to a mechanical thing, some disposable device of flesh and blood. In the same book I saw a Rembrandt drawing of a boy characterized as "an extraction of essentials." Well, the essence of a human person cannot be extracted as if it were a bicuspid or a vanilla bean, and Rembrandt, for whom essence and appearance were inextricably interwoven, would be the last to attempt it. If there is an "essence"

to be discerned, it is much more than a "system" of formal relationships.
It must be this person's singular way of being human.
The realization of this irreducible truth seems basic to an
adequate approach to drawing "from life".
"Without the heart, the essential is invisible to the human
eye," says Saint-Exupéry.

In this "Confrontation with the Human", I stressed, we are not
ever going to close our eyes to the humanness of the human beings
we are drawing, whether male, female, young, old, black, white or yellow.
On the contrary, we are going to keep these eyes wide open
and forget all theories, tricks, shortcuts and mnemonic devices
we might have been indoctrinated with on how-to-draw-
the-Nude... What is 'a nude' anyway?"
"Someone without clothes, what else?!", someone said.
"Not really," I answered. "I, for instance, when I take my clothes
off am not much of 'a nude'! Sir Kenneth Clark says that to
be naked is to be without clothes, but that the Nude is an art form."
I don't deny that the nude is an art form, but it is the art form of
voyeurism in which a human body, usually female, always young,
post-puberty, is conventionalized, smoothed out, depilated,
deodorized and depimpled into a tidbit, a fetish of sex-on-the-

brain. The English critic John Berger has pointed out how grand seigneurs and kings, to boast of erotic conquest and conspicuous consumption, had their beautiful mistresses painted "in the nude," often disguised as mythological personages, their natural nakedness camouflaged into nudity.

Isn't it interesting that nudes are almost always females—under thirty? Beyond thirty the female of our species seems disqualified from playing the nude. She must be simply either clothed or naked. Male nudes, although rarer, have a longer life-span. Ever since the Renaissance they have, when young, been brimming with virility, flexing their voluntary muscles formidably; when old, still muscular, they sit frowning with knitted brow like Rodin's preoccupied Thinker.

The female nude, whether painted or photographed, may stare dreamily into space, but more often coquettishly seeks an aroused spectator's eye.

As a "nude," she is a person no longer, pretends to be an object, a desirable sex-appliance. She has adapted herself to the ego-fantasies of the male as the potent owner/user of a passive object that plays its part as "the conquered." Offstage the object is more than likely to disclose itself, with a vengeance, as being a subject: "the nude" will throw off her disguise of skin and reveal herself as her naked self, demanding to be accepted as such, pimples, wrinkles and cramps included.

Models posing for life classes often assume that they are expected to play the nude, and are apt to take those mincing postures they believe to be charming, alluring, romantic.

I refuse to play their game: I focus on the feet with their awkward knobs and uncouth toes, on the rude hinging of the knees, the blue veins shining through the translucent skin of legs and breasts — that waterproof sheath of skin that encloses and isolates us so safely, yet which at lightest touch ("Oh, I'm so sorry!") discloses itself as a hypersensitive organ of communication.

It is likely that during this Confrontation workshop too we'll have some narcissistic model doing the nude bit, or even worse, one whom I cannot prevent from going into monkey-like acrobatics. Then watch the poor jellyflesh of breasts and buttocks atremble, revealing mortal nakedness, and you will see the human condition: "Ah, so that is the body you must grow old in..."

It is not the more or less ideal shape of legs, buttocks or hips that makes the model into one you love to draw. It is not the spectacularity of her poses, but the way a living psyche manifests itself in this human flesh. It is her spirit that stirs in the hand gesturing or resting on a pelvis, and it is this spirit that transmits itself to you as you draw and that either inhibits your drawing or makes it go all by itself.

Florence

Jack

The one on the platform has a face. And this face proclaims: "Whatever you may think, I'm not a body, I am not a thing! I am as far removed from being a thing as you are, who sit there gaping at me." Hence, contrary to all clichés of drawing instruction: do not overlook that face! Summarize it, if you must. Don't get so stuck in drawing the face that you neglect the rest, but do not disregard it either while trying to relive that body on your paper: without that human face the body is meaningless!

Some people are quite impossible to draw. You try desperately for hours, but every one of your drawings has rigor mortis, is stiff and lifeless. Often they are dead souls...

Matthei T.

Living souls practically "draw themselves," make every drawing spring to life effortlessly: suddenly the entire group becomes inspired. Even those with the least aptitude perform miracles.

Anne and Tanya

Let no one pretend that drawing from life is sexless!
Isn't every gesture, every word exchanged, every contact between
man and woman colored by their being woman and man, that is:
"Sexual"? The trouble is that we deny hypocritically the
inevitable and wonderful sexuality of this response, the pity is
that our conditioned reflexes make us confuse sexuality with
genitality, and assume that the latter follows automatically on
the former, as if we were Pavlov's dogs and bitches...

Susan and Bill

On the other hand, seeing/drawing from life over the years confers a curious chastity that has no connection whatever with cold puritanism, prudery or, least of all, morality. Puerile sexual curiosity simply becomes converted into wonder, and this wonderment increases with time.

The model is no longer an object, but becomes ever more realized as being a subject. That "model", that stranger you are drawing, is no longer either stranger or "model", nor even _a_ woman. She is now that particular Epiphany of the human - as - woman, and this realization informs every touch of your pencil. I see through her eyes... I feel her foot falling asleep...

Those full four days that started at breakfast and ended at bedtime flew by. We took our meals in silence, then quickly went back to the studio to study what we had produced in the previous session while waiting for the next to begin.

Carl M.

The young woman in her

ninth month of pregnancy sat there

peacefully as if in her own room, turned inward to the child

she was carrying, her hands resting quietly on her belly as if

protecting the precious life growing in it. While she was still

posing, a flashy redhead clicked in on her high heels, her face

made up into a provocative mating mask. She sat down, flung

her long silken legs one over the other, lit a cigarette, parted

her crimson lips, o-shape, and blew smoke rings, pretending

to be a piece of sexual hardware.

A little later when she came out from behind the screen and

started to pose, she tried to play the nude, hand on right hip, left knee slightly bent, head coquettishly at an angle, dyed hair flung back. Her breasts, provocative under the white blouse, now were not so firm, a little puckered. She had turned so that the left thigh was hidden.

"Could you turn a bit to the right?"

She turned reluctantly and pointed at the long deep scar on her left thigh.

"Osteomyelitis," she frowned. "Disgusting, isn't it?"

She was hardware no more, nude no more.

Software. Quite naked. Quite human...

"Not bad!" I said. He showed me his drawing with too obvious self-satisfaction.

"What's wrong with it?"

"There's nothing wrong. Your proportions are correct, the movement of the body is convincing... You must have done a lot of this...'

"Years and years," he said. "So what's wrong?"

"It's dead, I am sorry. It is not her. It is not someone else either. It doesn't exist: it is an average, a life-class 'nude'. You simply rely on what you know: you have a dictionary of learned

forms you know by heart. You recognize a foot, so you draw
a foot, an ear, an ankle, but you are not aware that a foot
does not exist. Only this foot exists, that is right before
your eyes! If you pull 'a foot' out of your memory,
you don't see this foot, and your drawing is falsified.
In the next one try to discover the truth from moment to
moment! Forget your standard shapes." That next one
was rather awkward, but it wasn't slick and mannered...

Almost all spoke of the one-minute or three-minute drawings as
"quick sketches", until I banned that expression, for it rests on the
misconception that a drawing done fast is a "sketch".
In THE ZEN OF SEEING I tried to explain the
crucial difference between sketch and
drawing. For drawing and sketching are
opposites. When I do a quick drawing
of a body in motion, the eye "catches
a joy as it flies" and the hand dances in
unison with the motion before the eye
without giving a thought to what
will get onto the paper, without a
"thought" at all.

My whole being is concentrated in what the eye perceives, the hand follows as its passive slave.

When I sketch this action pose I have a concept like "body jumping" or "nude reclining" and I jot down salient points or features of that body in a shorthand based on previous information. Sketching a face I also look for salient features: an egg-shaped skull, a hook or snub nose, a moustache.

A sketch is in many ways a caricature: it conceptualizes an "object". A drawing, on the other hand, is an act of reverence for life that may go further than Albert Schweitzer's concept of "reverence for life". For Schweitzer's expression still implies that there is a Me that feels reverence, while in seeing/drawing the split is bridged: I and life are not two. In the sketch the split between Me-the-subject and it-the-object is at its maximum...

One of the few rules of the workshop is "Don't intrude on the privacy of others!" Don't look at each other's drawings until the end of the workshop!
Not only does it not help you in your own work at all, but it creates exactly that competitive atmosphere that goes against the spirit of these workshops.
Seeing/drawing is a private matter between you and that which confronts your eye.

Sue.

Nevertheless... The woman who had insisted — nothing I said had any effect — on using a block of charcoal instead of a sharp pencil point, on "doing her own thing", came to look over my shoulder. All day she had stood there frowning in the direction of the model, male, female, chubby and scrawny, while smearing bold gyrations of charcoal on reams of paper, discarded on the floor.

Ms. B.J.C.

Mr. A.H.

"Yes?"

"You draw very well, of course," she whispered loftily, "but..."

"But?"

"Well, you sort of draw what is there! I can't find that very interesting, not very, uh, creative...see what I mean?"

"Sorry I just don't feel creative... not very..."

Maggie

"What I like," she said vehemently,

"is a free drawing, a bold, strong,

creative drawing."

I never argue... When next seen she was furiously blackening her paper with supremely forceful swirls, cigarette dangling. Then, suddenly, with some relief, I noticed she was no longer there.

Often I draw in museums, not to copy the masters but to converse

with these undying friends, affirmers of life. I converse

with the tender Corneille de Lyon, try to keep pace

with the effervescent virtuosity of Guardi, sit on a beach
near Honfleur with the lovable Boudin, watch Pope
Innocentius through Velasquez' eye...

The young mother nursing her child seemed to hesitate. But then she quickly threw off her clothes and lay down, her heavy body all freckles, on a heap of pillows. The baby, seven weeks old, had to be coaxed; then it began to drink; some milk trickled from the vacant breast...The mother was smiling now and forgot all about us. She was relaxed, naked, yet not on display, not a nude, but the human in its manifestation as female: sustainer of life.

The silence in the room was audible.

Hands stopped drawing, eyes

were large and moist, enthralled by

the simplest of mysteries.

"Why did you stop drawing?" I asked.

"I was completely involved."..." I forgot..."

"I was paralyzed..." "I've

never had that before..."

"You were SEEING."

A few days later I got this letter: "It was wonderfully moving: before I came into the room, I felt a little shy about modeling without clothes with my baby. Then as Jonathan and I proceeded, it felt so natural just to 'be' with my child, as if we were alone. I felt the group was embracing us totally, caring for us... Thank you very much! I can't wait to share it with Jonathan when he is old enough to understand..."

Sometimes when women — especially fashionable women — look at my drawings "from life" they wonder aloud: "But why do you have to draw such awful (or old, or flabby, or scrawny) women?" I detect an element of fear in such questions.

I am so much less fascinated by standardized prettiness than by the infinite variations on the human theme! The fat, the skinny, the flabby and the old are not awful! That which life has marked, wounded, does not repel but moves me.

I could draw it every day if it were not in such short supply, hiding itself in shame, to honor and cherish that which is neither contemptible, trivial nor frivolous: the human, the Real.

The first day of our "Confrontation with the Human" had been a demonstration of how almost everyone was indeed brainwashed and blinded by their "art courses", how the eye had been distorted and perverted into non-seeing and the hand into a compulsive doing and producing. Stiff stick-figures and stylized, even diagrammatic standard forms abounded. Legs were either stove-pipes or constructed out of ovals. Often too they were stereotypes borrowed from ads for hosiery. Heads turned out to be egg-like, featureless ellipses...

There was a point when I noticed that almost all were busily "sketching". Nothing I said had much effect. At last, a bit desperate, I grabbed a drawing pad: "Let me try to show you!"

Without as much as a glance at what got onto the paper I danced the drooping head, the listless arms, the tired, loose mouth.
I literally danced the movement of that poor girl's body.
"This is what you have to feel inside when you draw: dance the strutting of a leg, or its dangling, the swagger of an arm, or its apathy. Feel in your own body the apathy, the vitality, the tendency, the direction, the target of each movement!"
I even forgot that I can't draw while being watched...

Betty

85

MaryLou

"Don't worry about proportions! They'll come by themselves!...Don't sit there measuring! Draw! Keep moving...! Keep your hand loose!...Keep your eyes on the model!...Feel her movement in your own body!... Become that woman!...Scribble that gesture down! Feel that bending in your own back!...Forget the tricks you learned: SEE!... That is a diagram, not a living being!... See where the nose is in relation to the shoulder... the left foot to the right foot!...And that elbow to the spine, the shoulder, the pelvis!...Don't go over that again and again: that's not a line anymore but a mess! See BEFORE you draw!...Get pregnant, man!...Look again how this relates to that: constantly see the relationships...!"

After eighteen hours of drawing, at the beginning of the third day: gone were the stick figures and the superimposed ovals: They had begun to draw! They were seeing!

The star performers in our "Confrontation with the Human" had been the nursing mother, the pregnant woman near her term, a young black woman with an Afro, who between poses sat in her diaphanous kaftan enthroned like a Nubian queen, and, of course, the antique couple whom I shall call Mister and Missus Hogan, although evil gossip had it that they were living in sin.

Mr. Hogan was tall, very erect, and still preserved traces of a splendid physique. He had the bearing of a major general or a thoroughly defrocked archbishop, and a head that would have gone very well with such a rank. He was proud of being eighty-one. His beloved admitted to being seventy-two. She wore a flowery dress and a very red five-and-ten wig.

Mr. Hogan appeared first from behind the screen, strode to the center of the platform with great dignity, blinking his once steel-blue eyes — now almost off-white — and cried:

"Peggy, come out!"

Then he declared that at one time they had posed together
for very famous artists.
"They are all dead and forgotten..."
Peggy's entrée was more timid, lacked all self-confidence.
"Look at me," she said, the corners of her mouth down in self-
deprecation. "You should have seen me! I had a gorgeous
body. Look at me now!"
"Every one of these young women sitting here would sign up
right away to look like you when they are your age," I said.
The ladies in the audience signed up by nodding vigorously,
and Peggy, feeling much better now, asked,
"What do you want us to do?"

Peggy and Bill

89

"Anything you want! But would you mind very much taking off your wig?"

"Oh, I thought you would like it," said Peggy, pulling the carrot-red mop off her head and flinging it over the screen. Her short white hair sprang around her head like a halo. They posed together hand in hand, and as if walking in the woods. He sat in an aluminum beach chair with Peggy sitting in the imaginary sand...

"He who would pass the latter part of his life with dignity," I quoted Dr. Johnson more or less correctly, "shall consider when young that he shall be old and when he is old remember that once he was young..."

"Oh, we do remember, don't we, Bill?"

"Sure do," said Bill, "you bet I do, Peggy! Everything!"

"He reminds me so of my own grandfather," one of the women whispered, and I murmured back:

"He is your grandfather and my grandfather, and the Pope, the Nobel Prize winner, the Senator and the four-star general..."

They were indefatigable, and poor as they were (retired models are rarely very affluent) they forgot to claim their modest fee. I had to run after them with their twenty-dollar bill.

"Oh," cried Peggy, "I forgot all about it! We had such a wonderful time! Can't we come back tomorrow?"

"Absolutely!" I said. "We could go on drawing you for a year!"

"If we live that long", said Mr. Hogan, his white eyes narrowing.

"Still, it was great fun working again! See you tomorrow, God willing..."

Claske F.

Years and years ago— it was after our first swim together and the creek was icy... I saw you climb up the steep bank. You were blue with cold, shivering all over in the drizzle, your thighs all gooseflesh.

"There is only one you!"

To see that is to have become capable of love... The nakedness of a person you love is almost unbearably moving. To draw it confronts you directly with naked reality, with our

vulnerability, with the inescapable death verdict that hangs over us, the unknown period of our reprieve. You are overawed by the realization of the preciousness of that life, of the miraculous coincidence of its closeness, its synchronicity with your own. Familiarity breeds either contempt or... ever-deepening love...

"See you tomorrow, God willing..."
There is a belief in India that lovers whose dearest wish it is will be reincarnated together. I hope it is true for the Hogans

and for myself, for I am not at all tired of drawing
you after all these years... Let me draw you again!
Let your face imprint itself so deeply that I will
recognize you instantly...

When the marathon was over, not one of us was the person he had been four days before. Each one of the women had been little boy, black youth, ancient man.

We men had been pregnant, had been a Japanese girl and an Irish grandmother. Our muscles had been long and supple, then gnarled and knotted, our bellies had been taut and flat and we had felt them inexorably become flabby

Mr and Mrs. J.B.

B.H. and Liz

and pendulous. Our faces had been smooth and radiant, then grooved and wrinkled, but not a wit less alive. We had lived the human condition and knew it to be our own.

"It changed my view of life completely, not to speak of my conception of drawing, of art," someone said.
"A greater adventure than my African safari," wrote another...
"The perfect inoculation against the Playboy syndrome...!"

Esther T.

At the end of each workshop
I ask: "Would you jot down in a few
words what today has or has not brought you? Was it
worthwhile or a waste of time? Would you like to repeat
this workshop? Will you go on seeing/drawing? Say anything
you wish, positive or negative; make it anonymous or not. What
you'll tell me will help me in many ways to keep these work -
shops from petrifying into a routine. I realize, and I hope you do,
that it is a very provisional evaluation, for if something has
really happend in you, it will take time to ripen..."

Here are a few recent evaluations:
"Most important for me: your stress on relatedness. On one's
relationship with the thing you draw and that between all the
elements in each drawing. Indeed, what else is there but relationship?
Between creatures and between forms and their components... I
realize that up till now I have only thought of 'making pictures...'

"When I walked out during lunchtime— I saw the street, cars, signs, trees very, very clearly. I hope I can carry this feeling of clarity with me, also the sense of 'surrendering' to life, to a flower, a friend instead of trying to be in control."

"All too often I am facile, not even realizing that I withdraw from the task I set myself. Here I was able to fuse subject and object in minute passages. It showed!..."

"...I feel as if I had just begun to see. Now I want to see everything in everything."

"In deep awe for the immense and intricate complexity of a flower. Concentration is hard! And facing all those feelings of anger at not succeeding, haste, the racing of the mind... on this special day..."

"Why don't they teach this in school?"

"Stillness is the Way. As I drew the Queen Anne's lace, tears came... the realization of such beauty and design: What is man that Thou art mindful of him ..."

"I was beginning to learn the humility one must have in the face of a great piece of music or a leaf from the garden. I hope to give up my tendency to embellish, thereby robbing it of life..."

"It awakened a patience long forgotten. I can't recall feeling more at peace within..."

"I quit art school because I was discouraged. Today gave me back some strength and courage. I'll file what I discovered away for when I start to teach..."

"... a form of meditation that does not seem contrived or restrictive. Rather than shutting everything off, I can use every thing around me to attain some inner tranquillity. It is neither "inner" nor "outer" but of a whole, for it is essentially a tranquillity in reverence for beauty; it establishes a connection with all."

Such responses have been very helpful, and all that follows in this book is directly connected with these remarks, with questions asked by participants in these workshops and the questions I have been asking myself during the five years about my own experience with seeing/drawing.

One question that always comes up, a purely technical one, is:

"What pen, what pencil do you use?" As if it mattered... I pared down my equipment to a few inexpensive essentials (I may not be a great help to "the Economy..") that are no bother to carry around and that last forever. Most of it fits into my shirt pocket. I have – just in case of loss or disaster – two "Pelikan 120" fountain pens (I prefer the "extra-fine" nib). This pen neither spatters nor skips, and I find it most reliable. I also carry two Pentel 0.5 mm. pencils with HB leads, which are so thin that they never need sharpening. My favorite ink is "Fount India," a deep black water-soluble ink that, properly thinned, produces warm-grey washes. I usually thin it – properly – with saliva and apply it with my finger or with the sawed-off old Japanese brush I always carry in my pocket. "Fount-India" has also proven to mix admirably with solvents like seltzer, coffee and puddle water when needed...

As to paper: once more I sing the praises of offset paper bought from a friendly printer. It costs a fraction of the pads of equivalent quality sold in art-supply shops, is even cheaper than that contemptible newsprint which takes neither pen nor pencil gracefully. It is cheap enough to be discarded, which I find most important: one should feel free to discard a high percentage of one's production to where it belongs: the ashcan...

I'd prefer 100% rag paper, of course, for it is lovely to work on and keeps for 300 years. But its cost makes it too speculative an investment, as I am not sure that in 2300 A.D. there will be a public for my drawings, or even a public at all...

The rest of my outfit: the finest portfolio money can't buy. I built it out of two pieces of masonite, slightly larger than paper size, hinged with strong duct tape inside and out. Its carrying handle I fashioned out of my late dog's leash. This dual-function portfolio-cum-drawing board is closed with two wing clips that also hold my drawing paper while I draw...The last item is a little folding stool made of aluminum. Its original cost is unknown, for years ago I must have forgotten to put it back where it once belonged. Together with the portfolio it fits into an abbreviated, feather-light garbage bag of black plastic, decorated with a label of the Kyoto Grand Hotel to give it a touch of cosmopolitan chic.

This is the de luxe equipment most people can afford and that has served me faithfully in both hemispheres. It can, if need be, be much simplified: a few pencils and a razor blade, an ordinary steel pen and little bottle of ink, or a goose quill, if you don't hesitate to pull it out of a goose... Anything will do that will most sensitively follow your eye: first NEN to first NEN...

To explain these riddlesome words, I shall try to answer another question I am often asked and which is of real importance: "Why do you insist on drawing in line? I took a course in which we were urged to do the opposite, to work with charcoal and to concentrate on volumes, masses, weight..."

I am neither fanatic nor

dogmatic about drawing in line only, and if

I banish charcoal for the duration it is only because the texture,

the "vagueness", of charcoal is likely to fool one by producing pleasing

"artistic" effects that have little to do with our experiment in

rigorous SEEING. When I draw in line with a pen or a sharp

pencil I am compelled to the most intense, uninterrupted

attention to and awareness of what my eye perceives. It makes

it impossible to deceive, to humor or to flatter myself. The

quality of my line shows up every attempt at a cover-up, a

pretense. Looking at my drawing once it is finished, I

can't help becoming my own graphologist: I see instantly every

flagging of my concentration, every incompetence, every trick!

I found this immensely clarified and confirmed when some

time ago I became aware of an insight the Zen masters of

ancient China had expressed a millennium and a half before.

The Hwa Yen Sutra says:

"The incalculable eons are but one moment—
and this moment is no moment."

The 7th-Century masters had become aware of time as
composed of ultra-short time-fragments which they called
NEN, thought-moments of such flashing brevity that
for all practical purposes they could be called timeless.
The NEN theory is not easy to follow, but once
grasped I found it as illuminating as it is
provocative:

When my eye perceives something in the outer world, it registers it
during the first, immeasurably short mini-instant or NEN, in a
direct vision which is purely intuitive and cognitive, as in a flash
of profound insight into that which is seen. This first mini-instant
of direct apprehension or in-sight into Reality, however, is followed
immediately by a "second NEN", and with the same lightning speed
by a "third NEN".

The second NEN is a flash of mental reflection, of becoming aware of my intuitive insight, of this profound "knowing". But in the "third NEN", which follows just as rapidly, this awareness becomes "my" awareness: both previous flashes become integrated in my continuous stream of consciousness; are processed, as it were, in that region of the mind where reasoning, labeling, introspection—in short, ego—feeling—take over. The experience now becomes part of "my" consciousness and at once the Me begins to interpret, to rationalize and to draw "logical" conclusions from the direct perception, to distort the direct, "clairvoyant" grasp of the first NEN, and to imprison it once more in words and concepts. These cogitations, analyses and conclusions snowball further until the intuitive revelation of the first NEN is totally lost.

Another way in which the ancients handled their momentous discovery was to speak of a "first-NEN ego" which is capable of that pure intuitive knowledge beyond thinking of which Christ's words from the apocryphal Gospel of St. Thomas seem to speak: "You cannot take hold of it, yet you cannot lose it". They called "second-NEN ego" the awareness of this direct perception, while the "third-NEN ego" synthesizes both first- and second-NEN egos into that empirical ego, the "little self" we speak of as "Me". The "Me" is no longer identified with what this eye perceived, but has already "objectified" it, that is: it has made it into an object, a thing ... nothing is left of the first-NEN vision except its distortion. "Me" (which itself is the I-feeling objectified) and "It" are now at opposite poles. For the "Me" imagines itself to be the center of the world, and in its delusion takes itself to be the only really valid observer of the outside world, as a permanent and autonomous entity that is more real than anything else. A senryu says:

All the people I meet
make faces
as if they were going to live
forever.

What does all this have to do with seeing/drawing or with drawing in line instead of in blotches?...

Everything!! The discipline of seeing/drawing is that of BECOMING ALL EYE: that is, of seeing with the first NEN, so that each touch, each impact of pen on paper jumps from retina to hand — short-circuiting the interpretive machinery of the brain's third NEN activity, to land precisely in the right spot. In rapid but quiet succession, uninterrupted by thinking, these first-NEN transcriptions fall into place! My line is the movement from first NEN to first NEN. Or rather: these first NENS precipitate themselves in strokes and dots, and these strokes and dots form a perfectly continuous mosaic of first-NEN imprints which, together, become an image!

The very moment the third NEN (that is: "Me"!) is given the slightest chance to interfere, it takes over and the mosaic is disturbed: all proportions are off, the jigsaw puzzle no longer fits together... Either my lines become a meaningless tangle or I try to save the situation by applying my know-how of acquired tricks. I quickly shift to devices, to sleight-of-hand. I switch, for instance, from seeing/drawing to "stylization" or to "shading", or I tell myself I am "creating a design", a "composition", an "abstraction"... Or I succumb to the temptation to start "sketching." Whatever life buoy I choose, I am no longer one with what I see. I am lost, caught up in conceptualizations.

According to the NEN theory, animals have
first-NEN perception only, do not become aware
of it in a second NEN, and even less do they
integrate these perceptions into a third-NEN ego.
I see my cat watching a mouse. Her seeing the mouse at once
transforms her totally. It expresses itself in every fiber of her
musculature. An almost imperceptible shiver runs through her
skin, the sweeping tail lies motionless, the ears stand erect, her
face now is an "I see mouse" face...She pounces and "has" the
unfortunate mouse.

My own immediate response, my first-NEN perception, is as
SPECIFICALLY HUMAN as that of my cat is feline. When the
cat's image falls onto my retina, the reflex it releases does not
make me pounce. It makes, for instance, my hand trace a line.

Even before the image is labeled "cat," before the interpreting brain has processed and classified it, it travels through the psycho-somatic unit I usually call Me, "through the heart," to the hand that notes it down. "Absolute seeing" is this seeing in the first NEN, that takes place in the timeless instant in which we humans may intuit the Suchness of what the Eye perceives.

Raising my head I perceived for the first time
that the sun was circular;
Since then I have been
the happiest man on Earth.

(Rakan Osho)

Watching the man leaning against the bar, I found him rather interesting. I had already diagnosed him as being of such and such descent, such and such academic training, probably junior executive: third NEN!

She took a quick look and said: "Creep!"

What we call "female intuition" is first-NEN vision: "I like him because I like him", or else "He's O.K."... or "What a creep!"

First NEN, human style... female variety...

At the start of a drawing session, each time again, after all these years, it is the ego that strains and struggles and exhausts itself. The harder it tries, the worse the drawing becomes. Still these efforts are far from useless: they are necessary preparation, a warming-up for the moment in which ego gives up in despair and seeing/drawing takes over.

"I just can't stop my self-criticism", someone in my latest "Confrontation" workshop complained, "it inhibits everything I do, it paralyzes me!"

"Just let ego work itself to the bone! Don't worry about it! Just go on!"

For the moment will come that suddenly you find
yourself drawing, rapidly and surely, without
haste or nervousness.
All sense of time evaporates, and what seems an hour's
work sets itself down in no time.

Whether I see it happen in my workshops or experience it
in my own drawing: I do not know a greater happiness.

A warning : seeing/drawing can be a risky experiment for the artist still intent on playing a role in that subculture of egos-on-the-make known as the art world. That this warning is to be taken seriously is proved by two recent letters:

One is from an artist and teacher who had struggled, rather success-fully, in the various isms as they succeeded each other, meanwhile reassuring himself that not only had he remained "himself" in these changes of style, but had moved closer to what he really stood for. No wonder he was as confused as he was unhappy when I first met him as a participant in one of my workshops. A few weeks later, to my surprise, he turned up in another workshop I gave in a nearby city. "I just happened to hear about it..."

After the second workshop he continued to draw: he had found out that he was a draftsman at heart. He gave up both his teaching and his hard-edge painting some years ago and is earning his living as a printer. His drawings are becoming more and more exquisite.

The other letter is from a young woman who has been successful as an illustrator of natural science journals. She has developed her own style, and was recently commissioned to write a book on nature drawing. After some experience with seeing/drawing she now doubts whether she still wants to do the book.

"If I want to draw the way I really see and not be bothered by what others think of my style, how can I do the kind of drawings they expect of me for that book? If I ask your advice in my dilemma, I'll probably end up making this book subversive: not a book on how-to-draw-nature, but one on seeing nature!"

Yes, seeing/drawing is the "subversive activity" that runs counter to all the rules of the art game. Its "originality" consists in the return to your own origin: it is authentic, free from borrowed isms.

How I have found fault with that poor ego! As if it were only to be despised and to be annihilated at once. As if it were not an indispensable part of my life-process, that primeval narcissistic ruthlessness needed for growing up, for survival, that I share with ducklings and dogs... Zen does not bid me to "destroy" ego, but to "see into" ego, into its very relative reality. It is all too naive to

assume that ego can be "overcome" before it has had its chance to
develop. I must live and suffer through my karmic ego, that
psychological given, as I must go through kindergarten and college...
Until in the end you see that ego does not have to be cast out, but
to know its place, until it is "expanded to embrace all", as Suzuki
says; until ego and egolessness live at peace together...
It bears repeating that seeing/drawing is "a Way", a discipline of
deconditioning; that, like zazen, it does not "bestow" enlightenment, but
allows the sanity of the Original Face to break through all the automatisms,
generalizations, conditionings of the "Me", so that I may touch the "innermost workings of life"...When all labeling ("How lovely! How awful!")
all prejudices _ cultural and tribal_fall away, it is, as one girl wrote,
"...like learning to walk again without crutches, like tearing
down what was built up for the wrong reasons..." And another:
"It seems so simple to draw what you see, to strip away all artificialities...
it is as difficult as being oneself..."
If seeing/drawing is indeed "a Way", it is not a way to "knowing
oneself", but to "becoming oneself".

"I was discovering again things I knew as a child. I am shocked
    that I have drifted away so far from living as myself, but I
    am happy to have been shown the one place to travel to..."

114

And even more moving:"I have gone through exhaustion and despair. I had to deal with my assumption that nothing of worth or value can come out of me. I grew to being able to have trust in myself revealed, to feel free to let what I see flow out of me..."

It is comments such as these that make me go on giving these demanding workshops, for each one brings some proof that communication is possible indeed and is a crucial life-experience.

How on earth do you draw a crowd, in the street, for instance, with all those people milling around, not a single one keeping still for even a second? This is another question I am asked so often that in THE ZEN OF SEEING I tried to answer it with a hypothesis. For until I grasped the matter of first, second and third NEN I could only guess. Now that I understand it better I feel that the answer may be as helpful in drawing crowds "on the spot" as in drawing orchards or cloud banks. Perhaps what follows will serve as an answer:

I was driving through Amsterdam. As I stopped my rented car for a red light, I was struck by a group of people waiting for a streetcar on a traffic island across the intersection. Why I had the sudden, irresistible urge to draw these islanders I don't know, but I am sure that the urgency of the impulse is a crucial component of the process: the eye is caught, something clicks, the hand already fumbles with the pen in the shirt pocket...

The light changed. I pulled over to the curb, grabbed my drawing pad and started to draw the prim old lady on the left, then went on from there, "writing down" rather than drawing each one of the twenty-odd people, from left to right, without stopping.

All of a sudden a streetcar stopped, blocking my view. Not in the least disturbed in the watchfulness of the drawing process, I almost welcomed it, as if expected, and calmly drew the car with its passengers and conductor. I still had time left to go on with the houses across the street and the steeple in the distance, before the car pulled away. My island had changed. Some of its inhabitants had disappeared, others were still waiting for the next car and new arrivals had filled the vacancies. My hand kept drawing and let everything fall naturally

into place, in an almost unbroken stream of dots, tracings, lines, first NEN after first NEN. The old lady was gone forever, but the young plump one standing there now obligingly placed herself on the paper as if in animated conversation with the woman who was no longer there. Where a stout Hollander had stood, there had appeared a rotund Chinese whose head fitted organically the Dutchman's body.

What I had seen as I stopped for the traffic signal was a total image of the island with its mobile population in which each person was absolutely clear and stood as if frozen forever. Each one was seen in his particular relationship to the pavement he stood on, to the entire group. The houses and the steeple were not mere backdrop, but an integral part of this first-NEN vision. I did not — by sheer grace — allow any third-NEN consideration to interfere.

Each one of these people was sharply imprinted on my retina, not as a type, but as that particular being and no other. As the eye kept perceiving and the hand moving, the scene projected itself as if automatically onto the paper.

Nevertheless, Providence's jokes of replacing the Hollander with a Chinese of similar bulk, of providing the lady in the fur coat with a newly arrived but compatible escort, could not be resisted. For though seeing drawing is a serious game, it is played in perfect freedom.

Ever since, when drawing the baffling complexities of sea waves, orchards, cloud banks, I have proceeded as if drawing a crowd: without letting any fleeting thought interfere with my relaxed attention – concentration.

"Watching at leisure," says Satcho, "you retain the tracks of the flying bird."

Once my streetcar stop drawing was finished, I drove out of Amsterdam into the polder country that lies below the level of the sea, to see the flat landscape again under the endless skies over that tiny country of swamps and meadows. Again I had succumbed to the impulse to fly to Holland, to draw the landscape of my childhood.

The remnants of the land of Rembrandt and Van Goyen still exist: astounding vastnesses of green for this miniature country, of emptinesses that stretch pancake-flat and emerald-green under mountains of clouds in a boundless sky.

I sat down on the wet grass and started to draw the now sullen meadows and the charcoal-black cloud deck, when suddenly the sun bored itself through a pinhole and flooded everything with its brilliance - as in one of those biblical scenes of revelation on antique Dutch engravings. Gloria in Excelsis!

For years I had wondered what pulled me back to Holland so irresistibly. I knew it was not mere nostalgia for a country, for long ago I had transferred my allegiance to Warwick, New York. The few people I still know in my home town have become strangers, ghosts from a previous incarnation who expect me to impersonate a fellow they seem to remember, but whom I have forgotten. But when suddenly that drab meadow was bathed in radiance, I saw at last that all that draws me back is the magic of that cloud-filtered, waterlogged light that seems to radiate from the very center of things, that makes each tuft of grass, each cow, each grebe into a source of light.

"Here is manifested the unsophisticated self which is the Original Face of our being... Here is shown, all bare, the most beautiful landscape of your birthplace" says Sekiso.

It is this Northern European light, without which there would be no Vermeer, no Rembrandt, no Monet.

Can one be rooted in light?

I fly home to Warwick, and find myself walking a quarter-mile along the country road behind our house. The hills and hedges and fences are celebrating the rites of spring. Grasses and vines and meadow flowers are dancing in the wind. The fresh viridian of corn fields sways in gentle waves. A huge swarm of sparrows tumbles out of cloudless blue, a red-winged blackbird sits on top of the hedge whistling the Dharma.

"Does the blackbird have the Buddha Nature?"

"Neither dog nor blackbird has it, Master!"

"What did you say?"

"I said: The Buddha Nature is in the dog, Master, in the blackbird."

"I'm getting a little deaf," the invisible master said, "please say it again."

"The dog, the blackbird are in the Buddha Nature, Master."

"And how about you?" asked the master, raising his stick.

"I," I started to say. But as the invisible master's imaginary stick hit me, the cows behind the hedge went "Mu!" in perfect Japanese — quite remarkable for Warwick cows.

But then the hills echoed this Mu, and the sweeping tops of the trees repeated it, and the rippling grass and the clouds: the Ten Thousand Things, each in its own voice reverberated with Mu...

To come home from Holland, France, Japan, to find the whole cosmos compressed along this roadside should teach me to stop longing for places I have drawn, I have seen. But visions of some

Kyoto street, a beach in Oregon, a canal near Alkmaar loom up. Even in the midst of writing this they flash like living slides before the inner eye... The real roots are neither in country, nor in light! They are in these eyes forever bonded with all they ever truly saw with invisible ligaments... BELOVED EARTH!

"What we are looking for," said Saint Francis. "is that which is looking".

In Southern France, on the edge of the sea, there was one of these places that drew me back so relentlessly, an ancient olive grove, so old that the trees no longer bore fruit. They just stood there in that awesome beauty that may come to women once they have done with the business of charming, marrying and child bearing: that invulnerable beauty that becomes visible once the mating masks have withered away.

Each one of these ancestral trees showed
scars of centuries of struggle with wind,
lightning and droughts, those angel-demons
of a tree's destiny. Each one had lost
limbs in the endless battle; but still, their roots,
unyielding tentacles, bored deep in Earth, they stood there
on feet like lions' claws. Their trunks and limbs, assemblages of
buttocks, bellies, bulging muscles, warts, monstrous growths, were
a lexicon of organic forms. It was as if these ancient trees had
gathered a compendium in themselves of the generations of humans
that once had picked their fruits: brutish, wizened faces stared
from their branchings... For weeks I drew this miscellany of
life forms in their endless variations and combinations.

Last year I returned and found it gone. The bulldozers had
discovered it, had toppled the awesome beings, torn out in a
few hours the centuries-old roots from their earth, dug the swimming
pool for the sterile Condominium "Les Oliviers".
Two of the great trees were left standing on the smooth front lawn.

A stone's throw from our house in Warwick, the apple orchards still stand, blossoming in spring, bedecked with their juicy scarlet jewelry in late summer, to withdraw into themselves and stand there naked, in profound meditation, all winter long.

I draw these naked bodies, alone or in crowds, as I draw human ones. These orchards are not mobs, nor the algebraical sums of single trees. They are communities of which the roots are intertwined deep in the frozen ground, as are the human roots we so ignore.

To draw these communes demands extraordinary concentration. For each tree by itself is a universe the eye cannot fully encompass, the mind cannot grasp, the hand can hardly follow. Crushing weights seem to have blocked every impulse toward light and sky. Every contortion of each trunk, every convolution of each limb, signals the particular tree-mind that informed it: where to give in, where to resist, how to circumvent the forces of oppression, so that the young shoots may shoot indeed: straight up in rays that meet those of the sun, to suck their energy, to convert it into the explosive blossomings of spring.

But let the mind reel and give up in despair, sheer seeing will take over, and the hand starts to move with the stilled rhythms of the dance of trunks and branches, tracing each of these tree-lives in the cosmic pattern of their communality.

Heaven and earth and self
of one root
the Ten Thousand Things —
they and myself are one body.   (Zezenron)

When I no longer try to "organize," "compose," "express" what I see, but let that which my eye perceives express itself through my hand, rose bush and apple orchard become self-aware in me.

This is not a figure of speech. For to express is to make visible that which of itself is invisible. When, by sheer grace, my eye at last becomes as an empty mirror, it reflects what happens to be before it. The hand moves obediently — without resisting, in unison with this reflection — so that the true nature of rose or bird or face may form itself, first NEN after first NEN, on my paper. When the narcissistic, neurotic little self, exhausted, gives up in despair and drops away, I may touch that Ground of Being wherein both I and tree are rooted. The moment (nen, ksana) of seeing into Nature is that of seeing into your own nature. "Those who are steadfast in the face of multiplicity behold what light and grace reveal to them," says Eckhart.

When Soetsu Yanagi (1889-1961) lay dying, he wrote his spiritual testament. His lifelong friend, the equally famous potter Bernard Leach, translated it:

"Recently many works of art have appeared which profess freedom. Real freedom is free from the ism of freedom... When we become imprisoned by the clinging ego, we at once lose freedom and are subjected to un-freedom. The ego instantly sets about judging everything with the self as center of judgement... Lying on this sickbed I see that rather than those who have

'Talent' or 'genius', quite ordinary men who are most deeply, most spiritually alive have miraculously succeeded in creating things of great beauty..."

And therefore: the pain of seeing drawing is one's constant, inevitable confrontation with one's product in its inadequacy, in its falling short of "great beauty". For never will the form on the paper do justice to the wondrous vision in the eye. The bliss of seeing drawing is the instant of "seeing God with the same eye with which God sees me."

"Your drawings often remind me of haiku,"
    someone wrote to me recently.
    Really?
    Yes, come to think of it, those few drawings, among thousands, that I feel happy with may have something in common with the simplicity of Haiku, these 17-syllable Japanese poems that evoke some fleeting moment of seeing into the heart of things, and of being supremely alive here and now. What I mean to say can then be said with very little, and the empty vastness of space expresses itself as a single bird on a bare stalk or as a little bunch of people under the endless sky.

With every gust of wind
the butterfly changes
its place on the willow.   (Bashō)

The shell of a cicada
it sang itself
utterly away   (Bashō)

"If you want to see into it, see into it directly. When you
begin to think about it, it is altogether missed," says an
ancient Zen master

"What the reader, the viewer needs to understand — and this applies
to both haiku and drawings—is not so much 'art' as places,
seasons, moods, life itself," says R.H. Blyth.

It is deep autumn
What kind of life
is my neighbor's, I wonder.   (Bashō)

As each syllable in a haiku, every line and dot of a drawing testifies to
a quality of awareness, discloses the attitude of a human being to his
perception, his inner landscape ... All nerve endings are exposed ...

Looking closely
how lonesome
the cow's face.   (Bashō)

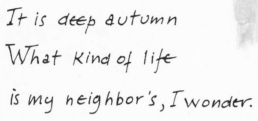

See how the fly rubs
its hands and feet,
Kill it not !   (Issa)

"How do you dare to paint those bamboos with red ink!" the
    purblind admonished the master. "Everybody knows bamboos are
    not red!"
    "That's true", grinned the master, "bamboos are black, right?"

Ƶ

The master Zuizan used to call out to himself:
    "Hi, Zuizan!" and he would answer:
    "Yes, Master!"
    "Wake up!" he would go on.
    "Yes, Master!"
    "Now don't you doze off again!"
    "No, Master, I won't!"
    "And don't ever let others confuse you again!"
    "No, Master! Never!"

"Remember the stereopticon, Frederick!"

"Yes, Master!"

'Use it !"

"Yes, Master."

I take my pencil and draw whatever

is in my field of vision.

A thousand years ago Hung Chi wrote:

Full of pure wonder
is this reflection
dew and the moon
stars and streams
snow on pines
clouds hovering...
from darkness all becomes glowing bright.
Oh see! The hundred rivers flow
in tumbling torrents
to the great Ocean.

The stereopticon, Hung Chi agrees, is within. So is the Kingdom, so
is the Buddha Nature, the Spirit of Christ.

135

"Clouds hovering"... On this bright day of Indian summer, the clouds are of white wool freshly spun, the maple on the river bank below our house releases its yellow leaves, one by one. On the soft breeze they take wing, turn and tumble in their flight, in their one moment of birdlike freedom, glide gently to their landing on the river, forming little patches with other leaves that preceded them that move inexorably to the waterfall, plunge over it, a little earlier, a little later...

The morning dew
flees away
is no more
Who remains
in this world of ours? (Ikkyu)

The clouds HungChi saw a thousand years ago are still hovering over our creek one of his hundred rivers. Ages before him, a living eye had been gladdened by these bright clouds and this stream. A thousand years hence – unless bulldozers and bombs will have flattened this earth – there will be eyes to see these leaves in flight on a gentle autumn day. The faces I have seen laughing and talking, mere shadows on yellowed snapshots, kept in old biscuit tins for a while, will have been thrown out long ago, blown away by a gust of wind.

She had been my neighbor but I had hardly known her. When it was my turn to sit by her bedside for a few hours I went across the road — "She may be going any time now..." — with my drawing pad. Most of the time she seemed to doze, but suddenly the pale eyes would open very wide and the ancient face stared at me with the faintest ghost of a smile, as if astonished to see me there.

I sat there drawing and it was as if I entered into a lifelong relationship with her, as if I saw her life in its totality. She was not in front of my lens but behind it, and so I saw her as the girl she once was, as married woman as clearly as now in the quiet dying of the light. My hand kept moving in the still room. The swishing of pencil on paper I heard as the sound of that all-too-proverbial "one hand clapping"...

"Life comes to an end at
the previous thought;
it is resurrected in the
subsequent thought...",
Shan-tao said in the
7th Century.

The young bearded minister did his utmost, eulogized according
to his how-to book. The coffin was being lowered.

The preacher handed the shovel to her grey-haired son:
"Please, throw in the first shovel of dirt," he said with mournful
courtesy.

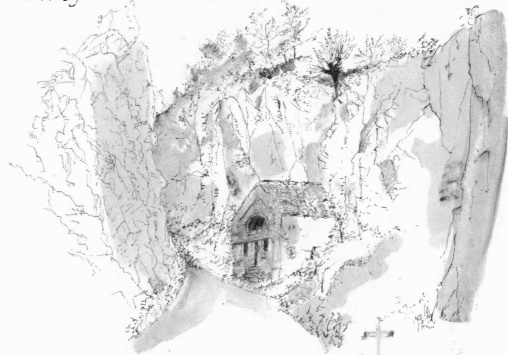

It struck me like a whip. Only in America, I believe, does one speak
of earth as "dirt"...

Are we the products of dirt? Don't believe him, neighbor! They
will not cover you with dirt! You will not return to dirt, but
to Earth, the sacred, the desecrated, the violated!

Where Earth is seen as dirt, the bulldozer is destined to rule,
to mutilate, to "develop", to "landscape" what is mere "dirt."

Mother Dirt...

"Beloved Earth, who gives birth to the Ten Thousand Things and to us humans who poison and rape you: Have mercy upon us, sinners...."

Grasses and weeds, apple blossoms and rocks, you and I grow out of Earth as the hairs grow out of our skins.
Skunk cabbage, field mouse and fly reveal stupefying marvels, loom up from Emptiness, arise and disappear in It.
"THE MATERIAL THING BEFORE YOU, THAT IS It" says Huang Po.
Yes. But to the unawakened eye that does not see but looks
"It" is just material things... The eye that merely looks is a not-yet-quite human eye.

The unawakened eye is closer to that of hawk or rat, apprehends only prey and enemy, a pre-human eye in a human skull, limited to recognizing and appraising in direct relation to its cravings and its fears.
The fully human eye is this same eye, once it is awakened.

FORGIVE THEM FOR THEY SEE NOT WHAT THEY LOOK AT,
HENCE THEY KNOW NOT WHAT THEY DO . . .

Astonishingly, the contemporary eye, blunted by a constant stream
   of photographic glamour and horror, when confronted with
   live reality has not yet lost all compassion and sensitiveness.
   It seems to be protected by an imperishable grace, for it is still
   capable of being awakened, of seeing the supreme miracle, that
   of sheer existence.

Then the bird's flight, the tree's growing, the babe's sucking, the neighbor's dying reveal the Tao.

Quite apart from all religion
there are the plumblossoms, the cherryblossoms! (Nanpoko)

Every plant, every animal lives according to its innermost nature. Only we humans— ever since Adam and Eve ate from the Tree of Know-How— have drifted so far from our true being, that to recover it is our highest attainment.

Know-How abandoned
just seeing and drawing
for better or worse,
I become: the mother nursing, the baby sucking, sullen youngster, black dancer, girl in love and old Bill Hogan flat on his back, his round parrot eye defying Death, become all these lives overlapping mine.

In the silence of drawing

hidden, yet visible, in each face

I see the Face of faces,

see:

that the plural of man

does not exist,

is our cruelest hallucination—

see that our Oneness is infinite differentiation,

see:

that the pattern of the universe

and mine

are not—two,

that what lives in me

is the Tao

in which all lives.

THIS IS NOT WHAT I BELIEVE

BUT WHAT MY EYES

SAW ON THE WAY.

Having become

all these faces, all these bodies,

a meadow, a flower,

a night moth and a cow,

A STRANGER NO LONGER

I AM AT HOME,

BELOVED, EARTH!

EPILOGUE

If seeing / drawing
is indeed a Way...
I don't pretend it to be
THE WAY
but since it is my Way
it might also be yours.

This art of mine
— if you call it art, if not
there is no defense
except that it is more
urgent than what
you may call "art"—
is nothing but
some tracings
on the Way.

I don't know where
I am on this Way
and no critic can tell me.

The stations are unmarked:
I only trust
that I am still on it...

All I know
is that between stations
I have to peel off
another skin of the onion
I call "Me",
skin after skin:
Not this! Not that!
Not this trick! Not that device!
Not that shortcut!
Not that pretense!
No! THAT IS NOT YET IT!
Maybe at the next station...
or is this the last...?

THE COMMANDMENTS

These Ten Commandments on seeing/drawing were revealed to me on a mountain, but also in a meadow, on a beach and even in the subway. For their revelation did not come all at once, but in installments, as it were, over the years, and always while I was busy drawing, and invariably on holy ground. But that may be because, while drawing, all ground is holy: unseparated from the Whole.

I. YOU SHALL DRAW EVERYTHING AND EVERY DAY.

II. YOU SHALL NOT WAIT FOR INSPIRATION, FOR IT COMES NOT WHILE YOU WAIT BUT WHILE YOU WORK.

III. YOU SHALL FORGET ALL YOU THINK YOU KNOW AND, EVEN MORE, ALL YOU HAVE BEEN TAUGHT.

IV. YOU SHALL NOT ADORE YOUR GOOD DRAWINGS AND PROMPTLY FORGET YOUR BAD ONES.

V. YOU SHALL NOT DRAW WITH EXHIBITIONS IN MIND, NOR TO PLEASE ANY CRITIC BUT YOURSELF.

VI. YOU SHALL TRUST NONE, BUT YOUR OWN EYE AND MAKE YOUR HAND FOLLOW IT.

VII. YOU SHALL CONSIDER THE MOUSE YOU DRAW AS MORE IMPORTANT THAN THE CONTENTS OF ALL THE MUSEUMS IN THE WORLD, FOR

VIII YOU SHALL LOVE THE TEN THOUSAND THINGS WITH ALL YOUR HEART AND A BLADE OF GRASS AS YOURSELF.

IX LET EACH DRAWING BE YOUR FIRST: A CELEBRATION OF THE EYE AWAKENED.

X YOU SHALL NOT WORRY ABOUT "BEING OF YOUR TIME", FOR YOU ARE YOUR TIME, AND IT IS BRIEF.

A NOTE ON THE DESIGN AND PRODUCTION OF THIS BOOK:

This book was drawn and handwritten by Frederick Franck,
it was designed by Elissa Ichiyasu, and printed and bound
by The Murray Printing Company, Forge Village, Massachusetts.